It is not fair to say of a pastor that he "only" has time for his own congregation because caring for the flock of God is certainly a time-consuming job. But it does highlight the fact that when you find a pastor who is willing to help and encourage other pastors, you have an unusual blessing. Over the years, I have witnessed Rob Salvato's care for his own flock, but I have also seen his willingness to invest in and mentor many younger pastors who needed his wisdom. And now, I am delighted that he has taken the time to put his insights into a volume that will benefit all pastors, regardless of their time in the ministry. *Lessons from a Church Planter* will be one of those books pastors keep in a convenient spot on their shelf and refer to often. Thanks, Rob, for helping us again!

Pastor Sandy Adams
Calvary Chapel Stone Mountain, Georgia

Rob Salvato has written a brilliant epoch of his experience in church planting. He has taken the time to go deep, revealing insights gleaned from his personal journey of faith and obedience. It is both rich and refreshing. I highly recommend it. May the Lord use this book to both inspire and challenge a new generation of men "for such a time as this"!

Pastor Ray Bentley
Maranatha Chapel, California

Planting and pastoring a church is one of the most challenging tasks in the world. As a result, every pastor makes plenty of mistakes. But many of these mistakes are avoidable. In this excellent book, Rob Salvato (a veteran pastor, church planter, and my good friend) shares the mistakes he's made along the way and the invaluable lessons God has taught him. If you are in pastoral ministry, do yourself and God's people a favor—grab a highlighter and read this book!

Charlie Campbell
Director of the Always Be Ready Apologetics Ministry
(AlwaysBeReady.com)

I began serving as the high school pastor at Calvary Chapel Costa Mesa during Rob's senior year of high school. I was privileged to be a part of his life when he received the clear call from God to the ministry and the joy of watching him take his first steps pastoring the flock of God.

Over the years, my wife Valerie and I have watched (close up and from afar) God work in Rob as a man, husband, dad, pastor, and church planter. If you were to ask either of us to describe Rob, we would begin by saying that Rob really is all about Jesus. He is genuine, transparent, sincere, personal, practical, encouraging, and edifying. That's why we love him so much. And that's why you will find Jesus, His glory, and the advance of His kingdom to be the heartbeat of this book.

Pastor Richard Cimino
Metro Calvary, Roseville, California

Rob Salvato was instrumental in my moving to Hungary in 1991 and has been one of the great encouragers and supporters of that church-planting work through the years. I am confident that anyone called to plant a church will be greatly encouraged by this story and will take away practical wisdom for their venture in this great enterprise that all believers are called to be a part of.

Pastor Greg Opean
Packinghouse Redlands, California

Church planting is no easy task. Pastor Rob Salvato gives some great counsel and practical application on what to do and what not to do. I believe anyone feeling the call of God to go out and plant a church will benefit greatly from this read.

Pastor John Randall
Calvary Chapel San Juan Capistrano, California

Lessons from a Church Planter is an honest look at church planting written from one church planter to another. I have known Rob Salvato for over twenty-five years. He was the instrument God used to prompt me to plant Calvary Corvallis in Oregon twenty years ago! Rob writes with an honesty that is both refreshing and extremely practical for anybody who is considering church planting or is relatively new to pastoring the flock of God. Written with a heart to pass on all that he has learned, *Lessons from a Church Planter* is an encouraging read not just for church planters but for anyone in ministry!

Pastor Rob Verdeyen
Calvary Corvallis, California

Rob asked me to read *Lessons from a Church Planter* and write a recommendation if I liked it. From the beginning, I found I was not just reviewing the book but absorbing it. There are so many things here I wish I would have known when I first started pastoring!

Pastor Brett Williams
Calvary Chapel Whidbey Island, Washington

Pastor Rob Salvato shares his ministry experiences as a church planter in a warm, insightful, and conversational style. Despite many successes as a pastor and church planter, Rob has chosen to focus on lessons learned from some of the mistakes he made along the way. The wisdom he has provided can help us to avoid some of these pitfalls as we reflect on his experiences and as we discover what God has called each one of us to do.

Pastor Bruce Zachary
Lead Pastor, Calvary Chapel Nexus, California

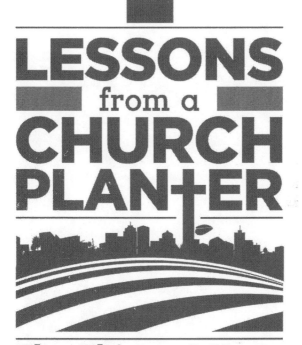

LESSONS
from a
CHURCH
PLANTER

The Things I Have
LEARNED
from my
MISTAKES

by Rob Salvato

LESSONS

from a

CHURCH PLANTER

Lessons from a Church Planter
The Things I Have Learned from My Mistakes

Published by Calvary Vista
885 E. Vista Way
Vista, CA 92084

First printing, 2014

Cover layout and design by Jamie Urbina

Editing and internal layout by Romy Godding

ISBN: 978-1-50076-403-6

Printed in the United States of America.

CONTENTS

ACKNOWLEDGMENTS

I want to thank my beautiful wife, Denise, who is my best friend, partner in life and ministry, and who helped edit this book, having lived through all of the content. Every day with you is a blessing and an adventure. Thank you for being such an amazing example of Jesus to me and to those around you.

To my three incredible kids, Aaron, Amy, and Amanda, who have graciously shared their mom and dad with other people for Jesus. You guys are awesome!

To my parents, Tony and Sandy, who have been so supportive and encouraging from day one of my calling into the ministry.

To the wonderful people of Calvary Christian Fellowship in Salem, Oregon, and Calvary Vista in Vista, California, who have been so gracious in allowing me to grow as a pastor and leader for the cause of Christ.

To Jon Courson, thank you for being a dear friend and mentor in my life. I am indebted to you for the time you have taken to point me to Jesus and help me see Him in the pages of Scripture. I am especially grateful for the way you, in my early years of ministry, listened to my crazy ideas and gently instructed and encouraged me in the ways of the Lord.

To Brian Brodersen, thank you for taking a risk on a young guy who had so much to learn. Thank you for being a living example of the grace of God and for giving me the opportunity to serve with you at Calvary Vista and to lead this precious church family when

God called you to move on. I am grateful for how the Lord used you to open my eyes to the nations and to the power of the gospel, which alone brings hope and healing to those who are lost.

To Richard Cimino, thank you so much for giving me my first opportunity at ministry in your high school group. It was an honor to serve with you, and I am privileged to call you a dear friend after all of these years.

To Romy Godding, for her expertise in editing this book and for her friendship and partnership in ministry.

To Jamie Urbina and Faith Amargo, great job on the layout and cover design! You guys rock!

And finally, to Pastor Chuck Smith. Although he is no longer here, his influence continues, and I am forever grateful. If I could, I would thank him for being himself. He was a powerful example of what God can do with a willing vessel, a great encourager, and he led our movement well!

INTRODUCTION

As a pastor, I enjoy reading books and articles about churches and their ministries. I have gleaned immensely from the wisdom and personal stories of others. Those who have taken steps of faith, venturing out to see what God might want to do and how God has used them to impact a community, always inspire me. Equally encouraging are the rare occasions when a pastor or leader is vulnerable enough to share with his readers lessons learned from his mistakes.

In the many years I have been in ministry, I have made mistakes and have learned some lessons the hard way. Therefore, the inspiration for this book was birthed entirely from the perspective of wanting to assist young pastors who are just venturing out: May it help you to stay focused and avoid the pitfalls that could lead to heartache in your personal lives, marriages, and ministries. I pray this book will be a help to existing pastors who are struggling or sidetracked: May it be a tool that enables you to refocus on your calling and minister from a position of strength rather than frustration and discouragement.

The wonderful truth about being a child of God, especially one who is fortunate enough to be involved in His service, is that God is faithful to cover our mistakes and misconceptions with His grace. He truly does work all things out for His glory and good. I am convinced that this thing we call ministry is more about what God wants to do in us rather than through us. I pray your heart will be encouraged and enlightened to the beauty and wonder of God's grace and love for you.

chapter 1

Keep the Main Thing the Main Thing

*You are not going to be truly happy or satisfied until
you are doing what God has called you to do.*

Tony Salvato

I will never forget that fall morning in September of 1991 when we loaded up a U-Haul and our little Toyota Corolla and embarked on a new venture of faith. My wife and I, along with our two little kids, ages one and two, were setting out on a journey that would take us one thousand miles away from our home in Oceanside, California, to our new home in Salem, Oregon.

Our hearts were filled with an array of emotions. There was sorrow for the friends and family we were leaving behind, as well as our familiar and comfortable surroundings. There was also fear because we were literally launching out into the unknown. My mind was spinning with all sorts of thoughts. I wondered if the people would like us. Were we crazy for leaving our church and the people who loved and appreciated us?

But like a mother eagle who pushes her little eaglet out of the nest that it might learn how to fly, God was pushing us out of our comfort zone—that we too would learn to fly! In the midst of all the fears, great excitement flooded my heart. Two years of praying and planning had finally come to an end, and the Lord was saying, "Go! Now is the time." We were eager and our hearts were filled with vision, believing God wanted to do something great!

The drive up Interstate 5 was long and rather boring, with stretches of nothing but flat land and sprawling cities, along with antsy kids and numerous bathroom breaks. Then the scenery began to change, and the majestic Mount Shasta came into view. We had entered "God's country." Everything was green and beautiful, with towering mountains and tall pine trees. I had lived my entire life by the beach in Southern California, which I do love, but I was ready for a change. I bought some flannel shirts and was set to become a full-fledged Oregonian—minus the cowboy boots and Wrangler jeans!

The first lesson God taught me happened during the beginning stage of our church plant, and I consider it the single greatest lesson of importance in my life. In fact, had I not learned this lesson early on, I am not sure that I would still be in ministry today.

Beginnings

I want to start by giving you a little history on my calling into ministry. I don't know where you stand on the whole subject of the gifts of the Spirit being for today, but this is what happened to me.

I was a freshman at college, playing baseball on a scholarship with the dream of making it my career. One Wednesday afternoon in 1983, on a rare day that I didn't have practice, I headed down to the beach with a friend from school to hang out. I remember sitting on the beach reading my Bible, wishing I had more time to get into God's Word. But with a full class load, morning workout sessions, afternoon practices, and a part-time job, it was hard to be consistent in daily reading or any type of study. My friend asked me if there was anything going on at my church that night.

I was attending Calvary Chapel Costa Mesa at the time and helping as a volunteer leader in the high school ministry. I told him that on Wednesdays, I usually went to the high school group. Well, he was not interested in attending youth group, so he asked if there was anything else going on that night. I told him about a service called the Believers' Meeting. I had never been to it but had heard it was a time of worship and waiting upon the Lord, giving opportunity for the gifts of the Spirit to be used. My parents had gone several times and had come home with some unbelievable stories of God speaking words of wisdom and prophecy through different people. To be honest, the whole thing scared me a bit. But lo and behold, my friend said, "Let's go to that. It sounds interesting!"

The meeting was held in the sanctuary and about eight hundred people were there that night. The lights were dimmed and the band began to lead us in worship. Periodically, there would be times of silence and waiting on the Lord, followed by a Scripture being spoken or a word. One of the assistant pastors, whom I had never met, approached the front and picked up the microphone. The Lord had shown him there was a young man present who was athletic, sitting in the back on the left-hand side. That was right where I was sitting, but I brushed it off because I knew there were probably other athletes sitting in my section. Then he

17

said, "You play baseball or softball. I want you to stand up." Then he just waited!

A warm sensation swept over my body—one I had never felt before or since—and I knew he was talking about me. I realized in that moment that God was using this man to tell me something. I slowly stood up, hunched over, with my mind racing. I was sure he was going to tell everyone that I was in some sort of secret sin (which I wasn't, by the way). As I stood up, he went on to say, "The Lord is calling you to give up playing ball and start getting into the Word more because He is calling you into full-time ministry." I was floored and couldn't believe it! That was the last thing on my mind at that particular time in my life. As I sat down, my head was spinning.

After the service was over, a woman sitting behind us approached me and said the Lord had showed her the exact same thing before the pastor had said a word. I kindly shook her hand and thought to myself, "This lady is nuts and obviously looking for attention." Weeks later I learned from one of my best friends that his mom knew this woman personally; he said I should take her words to heart because she was a godly woman and would never make something like that up. Obviously, the Lord knew I needed to hear His calling *twice* in order to believe and step out in faith in this new direction.

After that night at the Believers' Meeting, I was faced with a difficult decision. I knew God was clearly calling me into ministry, but I was also on a baseball scholarship at Vanguard University. Should I finish out the year and then quit, or should I leave immediately to pursue this calling? If I left baseball right away, would I be letting my coach and team down? As I was wrestling with the decision at hand, I decided to talk it over with my dad. He listened intently and then said, "If God is calling you to do something, you are not going to be happy until you are doing it." That was sound advice, and I knew he was right.

The very next day I went and spoke to my coach and the athletic director. Vanguard is a Christian college, so these two men approached my situation with godly perspectives and encouraged me to obey the Lord's voice, even if it meant immediately quitting the team. The athletic director, who was more determined to try and keep me on the team, suggested we start a Fellowship of Christian Athletes chapter on campus, and I could be the leader of it. But it was clear to me that I needed to take a step of faith in full obedience right then—rather than later.

The funny thing about the way God works is that years later, as a youth pastor, I had the privilege of establishing a chapter of Fellowship of Christian Athletes at Rancho Buena Vista High School, which grew into the largest FCA huddle in San Diego at that time. On top of that, in September of 2014, our church launched a second campus at the same school. I love how the Lord has a way of taking us full circle.

The next four years of my life were spent getting into the Word more, taking classes at a junior college, and serving in practical ways in the high school ministry at my church. I was quickly given opportunities to teach Bible studies at local high school campuses, God was blessing, and the groups were growing in numbers. I found that surprising because I had never taught a Bible study and didn't think I had the gift of teaching.

My high school pastor was a man named Richard Cimino—a mentor who became a dear friend, and remains so, even to this day. Richard started to view me as his unofficial assistant, allowing me to lead the Sunday night high school meeting and teach on Sunday mornings when he was away. This season of ministry was a tremendous time of what I would call on-the-job-training.

After four years of preparation and maturing, I was given my first opportunity to be in full-time youth ministry at a small church in Vista, California, located in San Diego County. I was hired by Pastor Brian Brodersen, who was another mentor and a friend. I spent seven amazing years at Calvary Chapel Vista, serving and overseeing various aspects of middle school, high school, and college-age ministries.

Growth

The Lord really blessed me personally over those seven years. I met my wife, and together we experienced the joy of ministry and became parents. On top of that, the church grew from a congregation of 250 people to a church of close to two thousand. Calvary Chapel Vista was involved in the community as well as in missions around the world. In 1989, the Lord led us to start planting churches in Eastern Europe and Russia, which was both fun and exciting. It was incredible to see how God was moving and to be a part of a church that was literally firing on all cylinders.

But with growth came more responsibility, hours, demands, and activities. Something new or big and exciting was taking place continually. We did crusades in our community and several missions trips each year. At the same time, I was overseeing both the high school and college ministries, which meant I was planning some type of retreat for one of those groups about every three months. The common occurrence for our staff was that we would spend months planning a crusade or a missions trip or retreat, then we would watch God move in powerful ways and bless the event. Once it was over, we would talk about the event for weeks, rejoicing in what God did. For me, it was exhilarating, and right about the time I would be coming down from that "ministry high," it was time to start planning the next event.

A Subtle Shift

In the midst of all the activity, a subtle shift was taking place in my heart. I didn't realize it at the time, but I was beginning to derive my sense of joy and satisfaction from my involvement in what the Lord was doing and not the Lord Himself. In rare moments when things would slow down, I would become restless and itch for things to get going again. In the midst of it all, a disconnect was happening in my heart. I still had an active prayer and devotional life (being an athlete, I was disciplined in that way), but it became mechanical. It was more like taking vitamins or eating breakfast rather than truly communing with Jesus. Somewhere along the way, I had lost that sense of delight and the passion for just sitting in His presence and listening to His heartbeat. Instead, I would read and go through

21

my prayer list quickly so I could get on to the next thing to plan or do in order to see God "show up," failing to realize He was ready to show up each morning if I would give Him the opportunity.

The Church Plant

After seven years of ministry at Calvary Chapel Vista, the Lord made it clear it was time to go and plant a church. A small community outside of Salem, Oregon, was the place, and we were being sent out by a great church. Like most church planters, I believed God wanted to do great things through me, so I headed out with lots of excitement and faith. But I quickly discovered that God was more interested in doing a great work in me before He would do one through me.

The first four months of the church plant were really hard. I have since learned that my experience was quite normal, but compared to what I had been used to, it was extremely challenging. Starting out with only a handful of families, it became apparent that this was a slow process—one that required planting seeds, watering them, and then hoping for growth.

I was devoting myself solely to the work of planting this church, but compared to the fast-paced, busy schedule I was used to, I was going nuts. To make matters worse, my buddies from the church in Vista would call me to check in and see how things were going. I didn't have a whole lot to report because things were growing slowly—the baby we called the church was barely formed. My buddies would proceed to tell me everything the Lord was doing in Vista and about all the events that were happening. I remember hanging up the phone one day and saying, "God, why did You send me to Oregon? It's obvious that You are still in California!"

The Day at the Lake

About two weeks after that phone call, in desperation and discouragement, I headed to a nearby lake to spend the afternoon talking with God (which was really a complaining and pleading session). In the midst of my whining about why He had sent me to this place and why it was taking so long to grow (yes, I was a real baby), God spoke so clearly to my heart. It wasn't audible, but it was the next closest thing—it was that clear. He said, "Rob, what would you do if I took away the church, the ministry, your wife, and your kids? If I took everything away, could you find your sense of joy, satisfaction, and fulfillment in Me alone?"

In that moment, I had to answer truthfully, "No." That is when it hit me—I realized the subtle shift that had occurred in my heart during those last few years in Vista. My joy and satisfaction had become wrapped up in being a part of what Jesus was doing and not in Jesus Himself. My identity was in being a minister of Jesus and not in who I was in Christ. That was a monumental day in my walk with the Lord and in my ministry.

A New Focus

The next four years in Oregon were largely about getting my heart back in a right place with Jesus, discovering who I was in Christ and allowing Him to speak to and mold my heart once again. We read in Luke's gospel that "Martha was distracted with much serving" (Luke 10:40, ESV). Jesus then said to her, "You are worried and troubled about many things. But one thing is needed, and Mary has chosen that good part" (Luke 10:41–42). Jesus could have said the same thing to me when describing my latter years of ministry at Calvary Chapel Vista. I had become distracted with much serving. Now, like Martha, I was serving God but the one thing needed was to get back to cultivating the intimacy with Jesus that had marked an earlier time in my walk. From that day forward, my passion became to know Christ more, not only through His Word, but also through the victories, defeats, and experiences of life.

In Acts chapter 13, it says that the elders in the church of Antioch were ministering to the Lord. Note that they were ministering *to* the Lord, not *for* the Lord. Ministering for Him consists of the daily responsibilities and needs that are a part of our calling. Ministering to the Lord involves sitting at His feet, listening to His heartbeat, being still, and knowing that He is God. It is coming to Him in worship and being amazed at who He is.

I have learned that my daily devotional time needs to be more focused and passionate. I have also realized that in order for me to keep the right perspective and priorities, I need to set aside specific times and days for ministering to the Lord. At least once a month, I try to set aside an entire day to pray and seek the Lord. I take my Bible and journal with me, spending the first part of the day focused solely on my relationship with the Lord. Only after I have heard from the Lord personally do I move into praying about areas of ministry that I have the privilege of overseeing.

In order to keep my devotions fresh, I mix it up every year by reading from different translations, incorporating devotionals, prayer books, hymnals, and other books to stimulate my heart and mind to see Jesus more clearly. Realizing that my relationship with Jesus, rather than ministry, must be the central focus of my heart has been beneficial, protective, and life changing. If the vertical relationship and ministry is right, the horizontal relationships and ministry will be right as well.

chapter 2

Presumption

When my boys come back, I come to see if they are big godders or little godders.

ROBERT DICK WILSON[1]

Robert Dick Wilson, a Hebrew professor at Princeton Theological Seminary, was a brilliant man. One of his graduates was the famous Dr. Donald Grey Barnhouse, who later went on to pastor the Tenth Presbyterian Church in Philadelphia, Pennsylvania.

Twelve years after graduation, Barnhouse went back to Princeton to preach in the old Miller Chapel. On that occasion, his former professor, Dr. Wilson, sat in the front row to hear him speak. After Barnhouse preached his sermon, Dr. Wilson came up, extended his hand, and said, "If you come back again, I will not come to hear you preach. I only come once. I am glad that you are a big-godder. When my boys come back, I come to see if they are big-godders or little-godders, and then I know what their ministry will be."[2] When Barnhouse asked him to explain, Dr. Wilson said, "Well, some men have a little God, and they are always in trouble with Him. He can't do any miracles. He can't take care of inspiration and transmission of the Scriptures to us. He doesn't intervene on behalf of His people. They have a little God and I call them little-godders. Then there are those who have a great God. He speaks and it is done. He commands and it stands

27

fast. He knows how to show Himself strong on behalf of them that fear Him. You, Donald, have a great God; and He will bless your ministry."[3]

Belief in a Big God!

I remember reading that story and thinking, "I want to be a big-godder too!" I think most people who set out to plant a church are men and women who believe in a big God who is able to do great things. That was definitely my heart in venturing out. Why else would I leave the comfort of my home and my parents? Why else would I leave my church family and friends to travel one thousand miles to an unknown place? Who in their right mind does that sort of thing? People who believe in a big God, that's who!

So we ventured out, like so many before us, to do something great for God! I will not lie. I had visions of a megachurch. It wasn't because I thought I was someone special or that I deserved to pastor a large church. I just believed in a big God and had only experienced being a part of two large churches that had had a great impact through their ministries.

I was saved at Calvary Chapel Costa Mesa in 1974, right in the middle of the Jesus People Movement. Pastor Chuck Smith would become one of my ministry heroes. He was a man who faithfully taught the Word and through whom God birthed a movement that swept the country. The thing I loved the most about Pastor Chuck was his humility and the way he kept ministry simple. Pastor Chuck was a brilliant man who studied to be a surgeon before being called into the ministry. He could talk intelligently about any subject, from sports to history to plant life or anatomy. His favorite subject was Bible prophecy. Pastor Chuck could talk about that for hours. Despite his brilliance, he aimed his teaching at the common man. Psalm 119:130 declares, "The unfolding of your words gives light; it imparts understanding to the simple" (ESV). Pastor Chuck taught the Bible in a way that gave understanding to the simple, and I felt like I fit into that category. His down-to-earth style and simple approach in teaching God's Word affected a generation of young people like myself who, in listening to Pastor Chuck, thought to themselves, "Maybe God could use me to teach the Bible to people as well."

A Life-changing Moment

I remember going to a conference where Pastor Chuck was teaching, along with three other prominent pastors from various denominations. Each one of these men were known for their command of God's Word and for their gift of communicating the Scriptures. The other three pastors gave flawless messages, perfect in every way. There was a beautiful flow of thought, perfect analogies, and clear points. When each of them finished speaking, the audience gave a resounding round of applause, filled with awe and appreciation at the presentation. But I think deep down in the heart of most of the pastors in that room, there was a sense that they could never achieve that level.

Pastor Chuck was the last one to speak. He got up and began to share, and although his message was good, it definitely wasn't delivered with the same degree of polish as the other three. It contained great insight but also the customary long pauses that had become a part of Pastor Chuck's trademark. In fact, in the days of recorded cassette Bible study tapes, there would be such long pauses during his teachings that you were sure your cassette player just ate the tape!

Well, on this particular day, as Pastor Chuck was teaching, he did something that I had never seen him do in all the years I had sat under him. He literally stopped, and looking a little confused, said, "Oh, I forgot something," and proceeded to fumble back through his notes until he found what he had skipped. That moment stood in such stark contrast to the other presentations given that day that I literally felt sorry and embarrassed for Pastor Chuck, although he didn't seem embarrassed at all.

It was then that a thought hit me. Each of the speakers were pastors of megachurches and had broad radio ministries with vast followings, but only Pastor Chuck had over fifteen hundred churches that had been birthed out of his ministry. I momentarily wondered if Pastor Chuck purposefully stumbled in his message, although I am sure he didn't, but I am so thankful that he did. Over the years I have had conversations with some of the guys who were there that day, and we all agree that Pastor Chuck's vulnerable moment was a turning point for us. We were once again inspired with hope and the expectation that God could use us, possibly to do great things.

Big Faith

Three specific ministries have shaped my church life experience: Calvary Chapel Costa Mesa, which grew from a small Bible study to one of the largest churches in the United States; Calvary Chapel Vista, which was a small church of approximately two hundred and grew to be a church of almost two thousand in seven years; and Applegate Christian Fellowship in Southern Oregon, which was a church of five thousand people in a community of only seven hundred. People would drive from all over the Rogue Valley to come and hear Pastor Jon Courson who taught with the same simple approach that Pastor Chuck did, and God was blessing it big time.

It was Pastor Jon who, in 1989, asked me to pray about moving to Oregon to plant a church. Here we were, two years later, in the northern part of Oregon, about four hours from Pastor Jon and the Applegate Christian Fellowship. I expected God to do something amazing. In my mind, that meant He was going to use me to grow a big church.

An Interesting Conversation

On our way up the I-5 freeway, Denise and I stopped in the Rogue Valley for a few days to visit family and friends, and I spent some time with Pastor Jon, who had become a wise adviser and friend. We met in a little coffee shop in the quaint town of Jacksonville. I told Jon about how I had been reading from Romans chapter 1, where the apostle Paul talked about the power of the gospel to change lives and how excited I was to see this happen. Jon shared something with me that I didn't give much thought to in that moment, but I later realized it was absolutely prophetic in nature. He said, "Rob, I have no doubt that God is going to use you because He is faithful to His Word, and you will be faithful to teach His Word. But here's the thing.

This church plant is not so much about what God is going to do *through* your life but rather what He is going to do *in* your life. I believe that this new church plant is God's training ground for your future."

Years later I came to realize the truth of that statement. God had to get me out of my comfort zone and away from the people I had come to lean on so that I would instead learn to lean upon Him. Our church in Oregon never grew to more than 250 people in the four years we were there, but during that time, God accomplished a deep work in me that became the catalyst for everything He has done through my life in the years that have followed. The important lesson I have learned is that every new challenge and opportunity given to me is the process through which Jesus is seeking to make me a better man—a man who is more like Him.

God Is Sovereign

Through the years I have slowly learned to not be presumptuous in my following of God. He is a big God who does *what* He wants with *whom* He wants and *how* He wants, *for* His glory! There are man-made ways and ingenious strategies to grow a big church, if that is your aim. But remember, anything you strive to *attain*, you will have to strive even harder to *maintain*. In the process, you will miss the work that God wants to do in your life, as His son and His vessel. None of us know the plan that God has written for our lives. He is looking for us to stay connected to Him day by day, each step of the way, throughout this incredible journey that we call the Christian life and ministry. As we embark on this journey with God, living in a daily relationship and communion with Him, His work will be done both in us and through us. The greatest thing that each one of us can learn is to live our lives in dependence upon God.

> "Yes, I am the vine; you are the branches. Those who remain in me, and I in them, will produce much fruit. For apart from me, you can do nothing."

~John 15:5 NLT

Let God bring growth to your church in His way and in His time as He grows you into the person He longs for you to be.

chapter 3

Elders & Deacons

*No man is an island, entire of itself. Every man is a
piece of the continent, a part of the main.*

ENGLISH SCHOLAR JOHN DONNE[4]

Our church plant started in an elementary school in
the small community of Brooks, Oregon, about four
miles outside of the city limits of Salem. The people
who asked us to come and start this church all lived
outside of Salem, so they hoped for a church closer to
where they lived. The school in Brooks was literally the
only place we could find to meet outside of Salem. The
location ended up being strategic because of its freeway
access. The church drew people from nine different
communities, some traveling as far as an hour away to
come to our little fellowship.

Meeting in a school meant that we were a mobile
church, so each week everything needed to be set up
and torn down again. The school was gracious; they
gave us a small closet to store our sound equipment
in. But the precious people who were calling this their
church home brought everything else in trucks and
vans. I think one of the greatest things about church
planting is being involved in the start-up efforts and
watching the Lord assemble a team of servant-minded
helpers. We had some of the best!

The men who served as part of our setup team

became known as the deacons in our fellowship because, in the New Testament, deacons are the ones who oversee the practical side of ministry. The first deacons were appointed in Acts chapter 6 when there arose a dispute about the distribution of food among the widows in the early church. The apostles instructed the church body to pick "seven men of good reputation, full of the Holy Spirit and wisdom, whom we may appoint over this business; but we will give ourselves continually to prayer and to the ministry of the word" (verse 3).

We were blessed to have such a great group of committed men for setup and tear down, that after about six months, I was no longer involved in the process. This allowed me to spend the extra needed time each Sunday morning in prayer for the service that day. Calvary Vista, our sending church, supported us with a full salary and insurance for three months. The agreement was that if the church did not grow enough in two months to support our salary, insurance, and the rental of a facility, it was my responsibility to spend the third month looking for a part-time job. But the church grew to about sixty adults who were generous givers, so they were able to support an income for me, as well as cover the weekly rental of the school.

It was amazing to see the Lord gather a team of people passionate about this new work. Having such a great group of deacons also allowed us to do some pretty cool outreaches, like church in the park in the summer and a huge outreach concert at a nearby college. Whatever the Lord put on my heart to try, these guys were up for the challenge. Some of them were builders so they constructed things for better storage and mobility. It was awesome to see guys who were excited to help and who were using their gifts for His glory!

Growth Brings a Need for Elders

As the church grew over the first two years, so did the need for discipleship and counseling, which was more than I could handle on my own. My solution was to enlist some of the men who were already serving as deacons by moving them into the role of elders. Whereas deacons help with the practical matters, elders handle the spiritual matters, teaching the Word and ministering to people. The mistake I made was not realizing that God had designed and called them to be deacons, not elders. I would try to set up one of the deacons to disciple a new believer and would find out after a few weeks that nothing was happening. They either were not meeting or the appointments were not going well. I began to get frustrated and started to look at these guys differently, thinking to myself, "What is wrong with them? Why aren't they growing? They should be 'graduating' by now and stepping into this 'greater' role of ministry!"

The Wrong Focus

The problem was my focus: I was looking at what the guys were not doing instead of what they were doing. I was like John the Baptist in his dungeon of doubt! Remember when John was stuck in prison? Two of his disciples came to visit him, and he instructed them to go and ask Jesus if He was the one or should they look for another (Matthew 11:3). Doesn't that strike you as an odd question for John to ask? It was John the Baptist who stood in the Jordan River and declared, "There stands One among you whom you do not know. It is He who, coming after me, is preferred before me, whose sandal strap I am not worthy to loose" (John 1:26–27). It was John, who, when Jesus came walking into the Jordan River, declared, "Behold! The Lamb of God who takes away the sin of the world!" (John 1:29). It was John who said to Jesus, "I need to be baptized by You, and are You coming to me?" (Matthew 3:14).

What happened to him? Well, I'm sure that John was thinking that if Jesus, his cousin, was really the Messiah, then why was he still sitting in a prison cell? Why hadn't Jesus gotten him out of there? I love the way Jesus responds to John's question. He tells the guys to share with John the things that they had seen and heard, how the blind see and the dead are raised and the lame walk. Jesus was essentially telling John to stop focusing on what He was not doing and start focusing on what He was doing and how He was working.

A Divine Lunch Meeting

At the height of my frustration, I was feeling overwhelmed and went to lunch with Dale, one of the guys on our worship team. Dale was a mature believer and sort of an old soul whom I appreciated greatly. He was full of wisdom from being involved in several churches, including Applegate Christian Fellowship. Dale was one of my go-to guys who would always shoot straight with me, but in a gentle and humble way that was easy to receive. Proverbs 27:9 declares, "The heartfelt counsel of a friend is as sweet as perfume and incense" (NLT). Dale was a true friend who would tell me what I needed to hear rather than what I wanted to hear. So as I began to unload my frustration, Dale just sat there quietly. When I finally finished, he simply said, "Rob, I think you are seeing this all wrong." He began to identify all of the things that our deacons were doing cheerfully, eagerly, and with the right hearts. He went down the list and reminded me of what a blessing these men were to our church. Then Dale said something I will never forget: "Rob, God has given us some great deacons. Let them be deacons and start praying for elders."

Tears fill my eyes as I write this because I vividly remember knowing immediately that Dale was right. I had fallen into the same trap as John the Baptist—focusing on what God wasn't doing through these men rather than what He was doing through them. The reality was, God was doing absolutely astounding things through each of them. In fact, to this day I have never seen a more dedicated, servant-minded group of men in the church. I am greatly indebted to them for helping our fellowship grow and function well, and for allowing me to focus on teaching, praying, leading, and discipleship.

When Dale said those words, God was once again speaking to me, and I had to go home and repent. I took his counsel and started to thank God each day for these men who were so faithful to serve as deacons. At the same time, I prayed that God would raise up and send men who could be elders, and that is exactly what He did. Within a couple of months, the Lord brought a few solid families into our church and men who had served as elders in their previous churches. They had a heart for people, were gifted to counsel, and enjoyed discipleship. Often they would notice the needs before I brought them up. Together, this group of deacons and elders would become an awesome leadership team.

Some of them had great practical insight into how things should be run and how areas should function and be set up. Others had great spiritual insight into people and the spiritual needs of the church. Twenty-five years later, I have a mixture of those same type of men who serve with me on the leadership team of my present church. I am equally indebted to them for their service and their sacrifice.

The Right Focus

Pastors and leaders need to be reminded that the body of Christ is made up of many members who all have different functions. Some work in the practical areas and often do the behind-the-scenes things that are vital to the work being accomplished. First Corinthians 12:18 says, "God has set the members, each one of them, in the body just as He pleased." What makes the body shine is when God's people discover what their gifts and calling are and then serve in those capacities with all of their hearts for the glory of God. We, as leaders, need to give people the chance to shine in the areas where they are gifted, rather than trying to get them to do what we think they should be doing. We also need to allow people to grow at their own pace instead of trying to fast track them into serving in an area where God has not yet called them.

Interestingly, some of the men who I had hoped would become elders eventually did, in God's perfect timing. Some of these men who formed the foundation of the church when we first planted it are still serving there today, years later, and are the backbone of the fellowship.

I am so thankful to have learned this lesson when I did; it saved me from years of frustration and kept me from potentially hurting people whom God had sent to be a blessing in my life and ministry. It also taught me the necessity of taking the needs of the church to the Lord in prayer before trying to solve the problems on my own. Through this mistake, I also learned the incredible value of having good counselors in my life— people who would be honest enough to tell me when I was wrong or improperly seeing things. Proverbs 19:20 declares, "Listen to advice and accept instruction, that you may gain wisdom in the future" (ESV). Proverbs 24:5 says, "A wise man is full of strength, and a man of knowledge enhances his might" (ESV). Lord, thank You for the men of knowledge, like Dale, that You have sent into my life.

chapter 4

Spiritual Warfare

The Christian life is a battleground and not a play-ground, and we must be on our guard at all times.

WARREN WIERSBE[5]

This reality—that the Christian life is a battleground—is such an important truth for the pastor and church planter to remember. Church planting is serious business, and the devil is never happy about someone wanting to do a new work in a city or town. I think it is easy to lose sight of the spiritual battle and the tactics that our enemy will seek to use to attack and discourage us in the work that God has called us to do.

That being said, I know there are those who are prone to see the devil under every rock and give him way too much credit for bad things that happen or for difficult people who come our way. I am not hypersensitive or preoccupied with the devil. If anything, I tend to lean to the other end of the spectrum, seeing things too practically and rationally, thereby underestimating the enemy. This tendency led to a problem in my life and ministry about three years into the church plant. To be honest, this chapter was difficult to write. But as I have shared my story at conferences with pastors, I have had many tell me later that they went through similar experiences. I pray that this lesson will help you to recognize more clearly the schemes and attacks of the enemy against you.

Weird Thoughts

Things at church were going really well. We were growing steadily in number, and the church was maturing as a body in their faith and knowledge of who they were in Christ. We launched home groups, and the youth ministry was going strong. It was then that I started having thoughts that seemed to come out of nowhere, and they were very discouraging. For reasons I can't fully explain to this day, I found myself trapped in entertaining them, which led me to a very dark place.

The first thought that popped into my head was that I was not called to be a lead pastor. Lead pastors spend the majority of our time in preparation and teaching. We often don't see results or fruit from our messages for months, if not years to come. I have to admit that there is a certain aspect of the administrative pastoral role that really appeals to me. They fix problems, organize events, and deal with things on a daily basis that often bring immediate results or bear fruit in a short amount of time. A part of me was longing to see quick results in what I was doing, which made me vulnerable to this speculation and probably contributed to this line of thought. I didn't share what I was thinking with anyone, but I did secretly mention to a couple of friends who were pastors that if they ever had a need for a "number two" guy, to keep me in mind. Over time, the feelings of doubt about my calling were cultivating, and I was becoming disheartened. The problem was that the random thoughts didn't stop there. They progressed.

The next notion that pressed my mind was that I was not called to be in ministry at all! I began to second-guess what had happened that night at Calvary Chapel Costa Mesa when God called me. "It must have been a coincidence. It wasn't real. The last ten years of my life have been a lie." I rationalized away the impact I had had on all the kids at Calvary Vista and in our community, knowing that it was the grace of God working through His Word and that He could have used anyone to do that. I knew guys who were better teachers and youth pastors, guys who were stronger in dealing with people than I was, and I found myself spiraling down. Once again, as these thoughts were filling my mind, rather than combat them or consider the source, I dwelt on them.

Paul the apostle declared in 2 Corinthians 10:12, "But when they measure themselves by one another and compare themselves with one another, they are without understanding" (ESV). The enemy of our soul loves to get us going down this road of playing the comparison game. The more I compared myself to others, the more I began to believe the lie that I was not called to be in the ministry. The discouragement and depression increased to the point that I was reconsidering what I should be doing with my life. Sadly, I covered up my inner torture. Every week I would get up on Sunday, go to the church and put on a happy face, teaching and loving on the people. Because God is always faithful to His Word, people were still being saved and transformed, and the church was doing great in almost every way, regardless of the fact that I was slowly dying inside.

The random, out-of-nowhere dark thoughts didn't stop there. In fact, they progressively got worse. I found myself considering that I had married the wrong person! Now, I should have recognized that as a fiery dart straight from the pit of hell because marrying Denise was the second greatest decision of my life, apart from following Christ. She is my best friend, my partner, and my lover. During this specific time in our marriage, there was no abnormal strain going on in our relationship. We were just a young pastor and his wife with two little kids and a growing church, trying to make it through all the normal struggles that couples face. But, with my hidden depression and vulnerability in my thought life, I did contemplate this crazy idea.

Let me be clear: I did not have my eye on another woman, nor was I tempted to stray. But the more time I gave to this thought, the more dissatisfied and confused I got. And don't forget that we were now living in northern Oregon, where it rains seventy-five percent of the year and is cloudy and dreary most of the time. This didn't help matters, especially considering I had spent my entire life living in sunny Southern California.

Slowly spiraling down into a dark pit of lies, I finally reached the bottom and thought, "Just kill yourself. What reason do you have for living?" I knew considering this was selfish and destructive, but the impulse would flood into my mind at crucial moments. If I was driving near a cliff where there was no guardrail, all of a sudden I would think to myself, "Just drive off the road and end it all." I remember driving on a two-lane road with a semi-truck approaching in the opposite direction and thinking, "Just veer head-on into the semitruck and end this misery." I literally had to hold on tight to the steering wheel with both hands to keep myself from reacting. Was I losing my mind? It was during this time that the Lord laid it on the heart of one of my friends to call me.

"I Should Have Had a V8" Phone Call

It was a gloomy afternoon in mid-May when my cell phone rang. I answered it and on the other line was a voice I had not heard in about a year. He was a very successful pastor of a prominent church in Southern California and a man God used in my life in an instrumental way. He said, "Hello, Rob, how are you doing?" I answered in the usual positive way, "Doing great. Things are going well." But then he proceeded to push deeper and say that he felt like the Lord had laid me on his heart and that he was supposed to call, but he wasn't sure why. I felt a freedom to be honest and proceeded to tell him all the crazy details of the four-month battle that had been going on in my thought life.

He quietly listened, and when I had finished, I waited for what I assumed would be a strong rebuke, or maybe he would confirm the thoughts and tell me I was not fit to be a pastor, having such an unstable thought life. What he said next blew my mind and changed my perspective forever. He said, "That is really weird; I was having those same kinds of thoughts two weeks ago. Rob, it is the devil. He is the one putting those thoughts into your head. You are in a spiritual battle. The devil is out to get you because God is using you!"

Have you ever have seen one of those V8 juice commercials where the guy hits his head in stupidity and says, "Oops, I could have had a V8"? Well, I had that kind of moment. I hit my forehead and said, "Oh yeah, I am in a spiritual battle against an enemy who hates me and wants to destroy me!" I realized then that for four months I had been completely oblivious to the war that I was engaged in on a daily basis. My friend shared a few more things to encourage me and then prayed for me.

How Could a Pastor Be So Dumb?

As I hung up the phone, I felt so stupid and ashamed. How could I be so completely ignorant of the spiritual attack? I took a walk to pray and talk to the Lord. I asked Him to forgive me and to teach me how to fight! In that moment, all the oppression that had been crushing me lifted. Like a broken dam in a river, I felt the water of God's grace and love sweep over me in a powerful way. My heart was filled with joy, and my countenance changed! I was so happy to be married to my beautiful wife and to be the pastor of such a wonderful group of people who looked to me as their shepherd.

A New Perspective

I have never battled like that again in my thought life, although I have experienced attacks of the enemy in other ways since then. But when talking about the subject of spiritual warfare, we need to remember that the battle is most often in our minds. In Ephesians chapter 6, Paul refers to the "fiery darts of the wicked one" (verse 16), and I am convinced that those fiery darts come regularly in the form of thoughts that Satan or one of his demons throws our way—thoughts of lust, discouragement, bitterness, anger—anything that will get our minds off of Jesus and on to something else going on in our lives.

I remember hearing a story of a famous preacher of old who, in his younger days, battled with his thought life. It got so bad that he began to doubt his salvation. It was then that his father asked him, "Son, tell me this, do you like these thoughts that you are constantly having?" To which the young pastor replied, "No, I hate them!" Then his father wisely said, "Then realize they are not your thoughts. They are from the wicked one."

Did you hear that? They are not YOUR THOUGHTS. This is such an important truth to remember when crazy ideas begin to fill your mind. They are coming from the one whom Jesus described as a thief who comes "to steal and kill and destroy" (John 10:10, NLT). Satan is after you, dear brother and sister. He wants to kill your joy, rob you of your peace, and ultimately destroy the work that God is doing in you and through you. Recognize the source of these thoughts and stand firm, wearing the armor that God has supplied for you. This armor speaks of who you are in Christ and the fact that He is with you and for you and in you. Part of your belt of truth is living in the reality that Jesus has called you not only to be His child, but His servant as well. He has placed you in that church and in that position and in that city for a reason and a purpose, for His glory!

Paul the apostle admonishes us in 2 Corinthians 2:11 not to be ignorant of the schemes of the enemy. Our enemy is smart, and he knows the areas where we are weak and vulnerable, so we need to understand and be on guard against his attacks in those areas.

Another strategy of the enemy is to attack us in the area of our strengths. It has been said that an unguarded strength is a double weakness. That might seem strange, but the reason a strength can become a weakness is because we are prone to leave it unprotected. We are not tempted in that area, so we think that we will never stumble. Any time that we start to think like that, we become vulnerable because those very thoughts can lead us to drop our guard, giving the enemy the opportunity to strike when we least expect it.

Disarmed Principalities and Powers

The apostle John wrote in 1 John 4:4, "Greater is He [Jesus] who is in you than he [Satan] who is in the world" (NASB). I love what Paul declared in Colossians about the victory that Jesus won for us on the cross at Calvary. Not only did He pay the price for our sins, but He "disarmed principalities and powers, … [making] a public spectacle of them, triumphing over them in it" (2:15).

Every first-century reader would have understood this picture right away. When the Romans conquered a city, they would take the leader and disarm him, strip him naked, tie his hands behind his back, put a rope around his neck, and make a public spectacle of him by parading him in front of the people he used to govern. That is what Jesus did to Satan and the demons on the cross for believers in Christ. They have been disarmed, made a public spectacle of, and stripped of any power or control.

A Lion That Has Been Declawed!

First Peter 5:8 describes Satan as a raging, "roaring lion, seeking whom he may devour." But in the life of the believer, Satan has been declawed and defanged. The best he can do is roar! He makes a lot of noise and tries to intimidate us and control our thought life, but "we are more than conquerors through Him who loved us" (Romans 8:37). As believers in Jesus, we fight not for victory but from a position of victory. Jesus has become our Victor so that we can win the everyday battles!

I close this chapter with the powerful words of the apostle Paul:

> Finally, my brethren, be strong in the Lord and in the power of His might. Put on the whole armor of God, that you may be able to stand against the wiles of the devil. For we do not wrestle against flesh and blood, but against principalities, against powers, against the rulers of the darkness of this age, against spiritual hosts of wickedness in the heavenly places. Therefore take up the whole armor of God, that you may be able to withstand in the evil day, and having done all, to stand.

> Stand therefore, having girded your waist with truth, having put on the breastplate of righteousness, and having shod your feet with the preparation of the gospel of peace; above all, taking the shield of faith with which you will be able to quench all the fiery darts of the wicked one. And take the helmet of salvation, and the sword of the Spirit, which is the word of God; praying always with all prayer and supplication in the Spirit, being watchful to this end with all perseverance and supplication for all the saints.

~Ephesians 6:10–18

chapter 5

The Next Level

To go to the next level, you have to be special, and I look for those special qualities in those players, those qualities that I think will translate to the NFL.

RON (JAWS) JAWORSKI
NFL QUARTERBACK AND COMMENTATOR[6]

There comes a time in any church planter's mind when he wonders how he can take the church to the next level. I think it usually occurs when the numbers hover around the same amount for a number of months, or when visitors come but don't return. The pastor is left wondering what the church could do differently. I am a firm believer that every church and church leader should be looking for ways to make things better, never settling for mediocrity.

When I hear someone say, "This is just the way it is, and we can't change it," I get irritated because I absolutely disagree. I believe that, where there is a will, there is always a way. But making something better and taking the church to the next level are two different things. Seeking out the first will bring blessing to your church and glory to God. Pursuing the second can bring frustration and disillusionment, especially if your plan doesn't work the way you had hoped it would work. I learned this lesson the hard way.

The Missing Piece

About two-and-a-half years into the church plant, we hit the point where it seemed we were not growing. As I surveyed the landscape of our church, a checklist ran through my head. The preaching had been good, even if I do say so myself. The school facility that we had been meeting in was a great location. Our children's ministry was top-notch. The ushers and deacons did an amazing job serving. But the one area that seemed to be lacking was in our worship. Our best worship leader at the time was my wife, but she was occupied with taking care of our two small children. My friend Dale was an amazing guitar player and excellent in sharing songs he wrote but not really gifted in leading worship. Our youth pastor was developing in this area, and he eventually became an excellent worship leader, but that was about a year away from happening. I was convinced that what we really needed to progress was a solid worship leader.

A friend of mine named Rob, who pastored a small church about thirty minutes from ours, would often meet me for lunch. I enjoyed our friendship and the great fellowship we shared. One of the things I admired about Rob was that even though his church was struggling to thrive, he had the best attitude about everything. Rob was not only a Bible teacher, he was a gifted worship leader. Prior to becoming a senior pastor, he had led worship at a large church in southern Oregon, so oftentimes when our church was hosting a special event or outreach, I would invite Rob to lead worship. He was great at working with our musicians and was a blessing to our people, and they would talk for days about what an incredible night of worship we had.

I found myself wishing that Rob would shut down his church and come be our worship leader. When we would meet for coffee and he would share the latest trial his church was going through, I was torn inside. I knew that the community he was ministering to needed a solid, Bible-teaching church, but I also couldn't help but wonder if his struggle would result in our blessing. Ultimately, I prayed for God's will to be done and hid my inner struggles. The last thing I wanted to do was give Rob an escape route if God wanted him to persevere and see the work through.

The Breakthrough Coffee Meeting

After months of praying, as well as becoming more frustrated that we had hit a plateau, I received a call from Rob asking if we could meet for coffee. As we sat down that cold, rainy morning, he shared with me how he felt led to close the doors on his church and was praying about whether he should stay in the area or move back to southern Oregon.

I saw this as my moment of opportunity and an answer to my prayers. I shared with him about our need for a worship leader and the many times I felt that he was just the guy we were looking for. I told him that we could pay him a part-time wage and would look to bring him on full time as soon as possible. Since Rob only received a part-time salary from his church and worked part-time at a music store in town, his financial situation would be exactly the same, or even better, if he accepted my offer. Rob was genuinely flattered that I would ask him to join our team, and he left that meeting encouraged, saying he would pray and talk to his family and get back to me in a few days.

My heart was racing—I felt like I was seeing the light at the end of the tunnel, and we were on our way to the next level! A few days later, I received the call from Rob telling me that he and his family were on board and excited for this new chapter in their lives and ministry. I was overjoyed at the news! Not only was Rob our new worship leader, but he was a great friend and mature brother who understood the challenges of planting a church and being a lead pastor. The following Sunday, I announced that Rob was going to join the ministry team to our church family, and they were excited. Rob didn't waste any time. He began working with the musicians and singers within our body, improving the quality of their gifts and encouraging them in their roles, yet with a humble and gracious spirit. The worship at our services definitely jumped up a few notches and the body was blessed.

A Different "Next Level"

Interestingly, although the worship at our church improved immensely, we really didn't grow numerically. What I thought was the key to progress and growth didn't work out the way I had planned. God had a greater purpose in mind. He cultivated and expanded our hearts as worshipers, and the worship experience became better focused and passionate, whereas before it was hit or miss. I think most pastors can relate to what I am saying. An effective time of worship can really prepare people's hearts for the message that will follow. When we recognize that people are not engaged in worship, the pressure begins to build within our hearts. We think to ourselves, "This is going to be a rough sermon." With Rob leading worship, those occasions became few and far between. He had a special way of bringing people to the throne of God, with an awareness of the spiritual battle, sensing what to say or when to pray, in order to get their minds and hearts focused in the direction they needed to be.

During the eight months that we were blessed to have Rob as a worship leader, our church really did go to the next level. We fell more in love with Jesus and became passionate in our seeking of Him in worship. I have heard Jon Courson put it this way, "Our goal should not be to grow big churches, but to grow big people." We became big worshipers of Jesus Christ!

I am reminded of Proverbs 16:9, "The mind of man plans his way, but the LORD directs his steps" (NASB). I had a plan but God had a direction.

The Answer Is Never In a Man

More than once over the years, I have looked to a man filling a position as the answer to a perceived problem. Psalm 118:8 declares, "It is better to take refuge in the LORD than to trust in humans" (NIV). Any time we put our trust or confidence in anyone but the Lord, we are setting ourselves up for a major disappointment.

Jeremiah 17:5–6 presents an interesting contrast of what happens when our trust is in people and not in the Lord. It reads, "Thus says the LORD: 'Cursed is the man who trusts in man and makes flesh his strength, whose heart turns away from the LORD. He is like a shrub in the desert, and shall not see any good come. He shall dwell in the parched places of the wilderness, in an uninhabited salt land'" (ESV). When our trust starts to be in anything but Jesus, our soul will become parched, and our lives will lack in fruit and blessing.

But consider the flip side of that and what happens when our trust *is* in Jesus and no one else: "Blessed is the man who trusts in the LORD, whose trust is the LORD. He is like a tree planted by water, that sends out its roots by the stream, and does not fear when heat comes, for its leaves remain green, and is not anxious in the year of drought, for it does not cease to bear fruit" (Jeremiah 17:7–8, ESV).

It is always good to seek to make things better and to be the best that we possibly can be. God is worthy of our very best, and the people we are called to serve deserve the best that we can bring. But the lesson I learned is that when it comes to taking a church to the next level, in regard to numbers, it is entirely up to God. Making things better needs to be our motivation and God will bless that heart and bring the growth that He desires, be it depth or width or both. God knows the number of people that we are capable of ministering to better than we do.

Jeremiah ends with a warning and a good reminder: "The heart is deceitful above all things, and desperately sick; who can understand it?" (17:9, ESV). When it comes to numerical growth, our hearts can be deceived into thinking that we somehow deserve more than the Lord has given to us. I love the story of the pastor who was complaining to Charles Spurgeon about the size of his church. The young pastor said, "Nobody knows me ... I have only 100 people to preach to." Spurgeon replied, "If you give a good account of those 100, you have quite enough to do."[7] The longing to have more people in our churches takes on a whole new perspective when we look at it through that lens.

A good friend of mine summed it up this way, "Don't worry about who is not there, just focus on ministering faithfully to who is there."

chapter 6

A Home of Our Own

Life can only be understood backwards;
but it must be lived forwards.

SOREN KIERKEGAARD[8]

It is not uncommon for a new church plant to have its beginnings in a rented school facility, YMCA building, or hotel ballroom. I heard of one church that held services in a funeral parlor. It was a crazy Sunday when one of those bodies was raised from the dead! No, that didn't really happen, but I am certain that people were distracted during services, wondering whose dead bodies were on the other side of the wall.

When a church is finally able to secure its own facility and have access to ministry throughout the week, it is a glorious day! That time eventually came for us. Right around the end of our third year, we were feeling the need to move out of the school and find a building we could use for our weekly men's and women's Bible study groups, youth group functions, and more. Our desire was to find a building located in an area that would give us a more visible presence in the community. With over half of our church attendees coming from the Salem and Keizer areas, we set our sights on the north end of town. The Lord provided a building on the extreme north end, right off the freeway, which would still give the folks traveling from other cities and towns great access.

I remember the Sunday when I invited our church family to walk through this industrial building and hear about the remodeling plans we had in store. About thirty people joined our leadership team that day for a tour. We pointed out where the lobby, offices, and nursery would go. I explained how the back portion of the warehouse would become the church sanctuary and where the bathrooms would be located. Although some of the people had a hard time envisioning it, I could see everything clearly in living color and was extremely excited to get started on the project.

The landlord generously gave us two months free rent, which we hoped would be enough time to get the permits and to build out the classrooms, bathrooms, and sanctuary. The Lord had also blessed us with a surplus of money to use for all the tenant improvements and to purchase new chairs. Everything seemed to be falling into place. Yet, there was one problem—me. I lacked faith in God to provide for the process.

Lack of Faith

I was convinced there was no way our church would be able to afford rent on the existing school and the new building at the same time. In my mind, we had no option but to complete all of the construction necessary within the two-month timeframe of free rent. Consequently, I set a grueling schedule for me and for the men in our church who had volunteered their help.

God had blessed us with men who were gifted in the trades and who had building and construction skills. But all of these men worked full time, which meant we were going to have to do the construction project at night after work. On top of that, my wife was seven months pregnant with our third child. So every day I headed to the church around 8 a.m. and spent the morning hours doing my normal tasks. Then there was demo work to do on the new building, and the construction guys would give me a list of materials to pick up at the local Home Depot for construction projects that night.

The guys would begin to show up in the late afternoon, I would buy pizza or sandwiches, and we would work till midnight almost every day but Sunday. Most of the men came two or three times a week, but a brother named Dennis, who was the lead contractor on the project, and I worked fifteen-hour days, six days a week. Did I mention that my wife was seven months pregnant when we began this project? During this process, I ignored a pattern I had set for my life several years earlier.

It was at a Preach the Word Conference I had attended where I heard Pastor David Jeremiah describe his view of relationships. He said, "I am first of all a person who is living in a relationship with Jesus Christ. Then, I am a partner in marriage with my wife, followed by the fact that I am a parent to my children, and finally, I am a pastor."

When I heard those words, I was determined to set that as the model through which I would navigate my way through life and ministry. I was first and foremost a person living in a personal relationship with Jesus. My relationship with Him was to be the most important and through which all the other relationships were to be stimulated and inspired by. Second, I was in a wonderful marriage relationship with my beautiful wife and my closet confidante. After my relationship with her, I was a dad to my amazing kids who were full of life and creativity. Finally, I was a pastor to a precious flock of people.

In my mind, most pastors' wives and their kids sacrifice enough in just the normal day-to-day aspects of ministry. Hurting sheep don't often think about the pastor's family when are dealing with an issue or a crisis. They just want their pastor to help them through the problem or issue at hand. For years, I felt like I had done a good job of keeping my relationship with Jesus central and my relationship with my family before the ministry. I had seen enough pastors put their ministries ahead of their families to the point where the wife felt like ministry was his mistress and the kids hated the church because it had dad's attention and affection. I was determined not to go that route.

But now, in the midst of a building project, I had lost my way. Needless to say, the grueling schedule took a toll on my marriage and caused my family to feel neglected because I had put the church ahead of them.

It's Just for a Season

My argument for changing my priorities and allowing my model of person, partner, parent, and pastor to become inverted was, "It's just for a season." The problem with seasons is that they are usually longer than you think and they can produce bad habits that quickly become the norm. Any time you sacrifice your family for a reason, there are going to be repercussions. Our situation was no different. My wife and I grew distant, and she was beginning to resent me. I had left her at home to take care of every other aspect of our lives, and she was good at it. So good, in fact, that she could function pretty well independent of me, which only gave me an excuse to plunge deeper into the project and made her feel more comfortable taking care of things on her own. When this season of busyness was finally over, it took months to repair the damage and rebuild our relationship.

God's Provision

Like most construction projects, especially those on an aggressive timeline, it ended up taking longer to complete than we had anticipated. There were the normal inspection issues and corrections, back orders, and challenges. When everything was said and done, the eight-week project turned into fourteen weeks! We wound up paying rent on the new building and the school at the same time after all. Money was flowing out of our account left and right, and as I wrote checks, I hoped and prayed they would not bounce. But guess what happened?

God faithfully provided! We were able to pay both rents, pay staff salaries, pay for all of the supplies, and when we finally had our first service in the new building, we had more money in the bank than we could believe! It was enough to cover all of our expenses for two full months. I was absolutely blown away! God was graciously teaching me that when He is in something, He will provide. In hindsight, we could have kept a more reasonable work schedule and not have killed ourselves in the process or sacrificed our families, and we would have still finished in the fourteen-week timeframe had I just trusted the Lord to provide for the work He had called us to do.

In his book, *A Quest for More: Living for Something Bigger than You,* Paul David Tripp declares, "It is a sweet thing that we serve a dissatisfied God who has destinations in mind for us that we would never choose for ourselves. It really is a good thing that He will not be satisfied until He has gotten us exactly where He created us and re-created us to be."[9] The pages of Scripture are full of situations where God supplied what the people were lacking. Why should we believe that things would be different today? Once we have clear, confirmed direction from the Lord on something, we need to step out, believing that He is going to lead and provide.

The Lord knows what He is doing and is going to get you to the desired destination. The question is, will you go with the flow or spend the majority of your time swimming against the current? We all know that that choice is exhausting, and eventually you end up where the current wants to take you. I have learned that it is much better to just go with the flow of God's grace and Spirit, trusting Him to take care of the details and get me to the journey's end.

Pastor Chuck Swindoll said it best: "We must cease striving and trust God to provide what He thinks is best and in whatever time He chooses to make it available. But this kind of trusting doesn't come naturally. It's a spiritual crisis of the will in which we must choose to exercise faith."[10]

There will be times when God asks you to do something that doesn't make any sense logically; but if He has given you and your leadership confirmation, the best thing you can do is have a "spiritual crisis of the will" and completely trust Him! God is going to do what He intends to do. The question is: are you going to enjoy it, or are you going to worry and stress out and make yourself and everyone around you miserable? God loves to do things in our lives and churches that we can't explain because that is when He gets the glory!

chapter 7

Money Ball

Christian leadership always lives at the intersection of God, assignment and a person.

CRAWFORD LORITTS[11]

You have all heard the saying, "Beggars can't be choosers." In the early years of church planting, I think many pastors feel like beggars when it comes to finding help for the ministry. The criteria are minimal: Are they saved? Are they breathing? Are they willing? Can they pass a background check? If the answer to all of these questions is yes, then we can use them. But when you are fortunate enough to hire staff, your criteria can become more narrow and focused in your approach. You are going to be paying this person after all, right?

The Philosophy of Money Ball

The two churches I have pastored have been located in areas that are primarily made up of blue-collar, hardworking people who live month-to-month. What our people lacked in the area of giving financially, they made up for in the area of service. Our churches have always had a twenty-five to thirty percent volunteer ratio rather than the usual five to ten percent in many churches.

Being a church with a smaller budget has always made hiring new people to fill positions challenging. I liken our approach to hiring similar to the Oakland A's philosophy depicted in the movie *Money Ball*. In the arena of big league baseball, you have teams like the New York Yankees who can go out and buy an All-Star to fill any spot on the roster. Money is usually not an issue because of their huge payroll, so they end up with a roster full of high-priced All-Stars and huge expectations.

Some ministries are able to function in a similar way. God has placed them in more affluent areas where the giving is higher, or He has enabled them to experience some unusual growth that allows for them to have a great surplus to use in building their team. So when they need to find a new person to fill a role, they can afford to shop around and find the All-Stars out there. Sometimes that person serves in a smaller church, and they are able to offer them a pretty package to become a part of their team.

In the baseball world, you also have teams like the Oakland A's who practice what has come to be known as "money ball." The philosophy of the Oakland A's was to build a strong farm system, seeing the potential in players before anyone else did. The Oakland A's were also forced to take chances with players by giving them opportunities to play at the big league level before they were ready. While some teams are filled with polished professionals, the A's were filled with young players eager to make their mark in the world and were extremely appreciative of being given the opportunity. Many of them, however, knew themselves that they were not ready. The interesting thing is, some of those players would prove themselves, and when their contracts were up, they would be signed as free agents by teams like the Yankees.

The philosophy of ministry at my current church, Calvary Vista, has been a lot like that of the Oakland A's. Our low budget forced us to be a church that hired from within, rather than going out and looking for the All-Star to fill a role. We hired young people with great hearts who were teachable and eager to serve.

Patience Is a Virtue?

Hiring young, inexperienced people meant that we would be forced to be patient and realize that these new leaders in training were going to be learning on the job and potentially making a lot of mistakes. For instance, when we would hire a new youth pastor who had no experience, I realized that it was going to take a good year for him to figure out everything that was involved in being an effective youth pastor. In spite of this, the Lord has consistently blessed us with strong youth ministries and guys who would later become great youth pastors. The hard thing was learning to be patient and give them time to grow.

I have always had a staunch work ethic. It has helped me to excel in school, sports, and in the jobs I had before entering into the ministry. Being a self-starter, my philosophy was to be the hardest working guy on the team or in the company. My current number one assistant pastor is wired the same way. Steve joined our team after spending years in the business world as an executive for a large lumber supply company before running his own successful business for over fifteen years. Steve left all of that and took a major pay cut to join the team as my right-hand man. Steve is a man's man type of guy, a rational and practical thinker with good common sense. He is as hard of a worker as I have ever seen in my life. Steve and I are similar in age and come from family backgrounds where our fathers were also hard-working men.

Steve and I were now forced to oversee and work with young guys, many who had never had a full-time job, and some who had not graduated from college. It has been said that patience is a virtue, but I would add to that, being patient is easier said than done! Not only did Steve and I have to learn how to let guys grow and develop, we also had to learn to appreciate their approach to life and way of thinking. It took time, but we discovered that their differences were actually a blessing in disguise. I think we have learned as much from them as they have learned from us. We have been blessed to see many of these young men develop into incredible ministers and leaders. Like the Oakland A's, we have seen many of them move on to join larger ministry teams who, like the Yankees, were looking for an All-Star to fill a ministry need.

In retrospect, I also think our inability to pay guys what they were worth worked in God's favor. Several of them took great steps of faith to go and plant their own churches in different parts of the country and the world. To date, thirty-one churches have been birthed and all of them have impacted their communities.

A Full Plate

In the early years of our partnership, Steve and I took the approach that we were training guys to be pastors. Our emphasis was to teach them responsibility and create routines that would help them grow in the practical areas of time management, being self-starters, and being servant-minded. I had gone through a similar style of training and saw the benefits it had played in my own life.

When I was first hired as a youth pastor, I quickly discovered that my role would stretch far beyond ministering to kids. In the early years of that first position, I was also responsible for cleaning bathrooms, washing windows, vacuuming the classrooms and the sanctuary, setting up chairs in the sanctuary, and mowing the yard outside the church building. At first I wrestled with doing what I thought to be menial tasks, but eventually I saw that God was using that time in my life to develop a servant's heart. It has been said, "You know if you have a servant's heart by the way you react when someone treats you like a servant." Having these different responsibilities also forced me to learn how to manage my time and multitask, which were valuable lessons for me to grasp and would become a catalyst in my training technique.

I am a big believer in putting more on people's plates than they can handle because I have found that most people will rarely ever ask for more to do. But when someone has more to do than they have time in the day to accomplish, three things can happen. First, they can learn how to trust God to meet them in those places where they didn't have the time to prepare. Second, they can learn how to delegate and find others to help them fulfill the task that is required. Third, they can learn how to say, "I can't handle all of this; I need help." I have found the whole exercise helpful for guys to discovering what their strengths and weaknesses are.

For that reason, early on, everyone on our pastoral staff was required to spend two hours each week doing janitorial duties for our church and for our K-12th school. Most of the guys really grew from this structure, even though some of them wrestled like I had with being required to do janitorial work when they were hired to be pastors. They learned to juggle a wide variety of responsibilities and many of them became overachievers.

A Change of Perspective

This system worked very well for several years, and we were seeing some incredible results in the lives of the men and women we were leading. I think it's safe to say that many of the guys surprised themselves and us in what they were able to accomplish.

But our whole system and philosophy was greatly challenged when we hired two guys who were extremely artistic. One of the guys was a phenomenal musician and songwriter who has gone on to lead worship at two larger churches. The other was a gifted artist who would draw and paint incredible pictures. The thing about artistic, right-brain types is that they think and approach life differently. Some, though not all, struggle with being organized and being on time, which was definitely the case with these two individuals.

The mistake we made was not recognizing the fact that they were not going to fit into the box that we had created for ministry. Unfortunately, they both left Calvary Vista sooner that we had hoped and did not achieve their full ministry potential under our leadership.

After seeing one of these young men leave our team prematurely, I sat down with Steve and told him that I thought we had to re-evaluate the way we worked with and treated the artistic guys. Although our expectations would stay high for them in the area of spiritual matters and character, we needed to lower our expectations and offer more flexibility in areas like time management and responsibilities. We had come to realize that many artistic types do their best work between the hours of 12:00 a.m. to 3:00 a.m., so requiring them to be at work at 8:30 a.m. every day was unreasonable.

Now, we try to create an environment of greater flexibility with artistic employees that will lend itself to their creativity, and as a result, benefit our church body. I love the line in the movie *Chariots of Fire*, where Eric Liddell's sister chides Eric for wasting his time with running when God had called him to be a missionary. His response is classic and provides a great lesson. He declared, "I believe God made me for a purpose, but He also made me fast. And when I run, I feel His pleasure."

I realize now that God has created each of us to run in a particular area and in a certain way. It is beautiful to watch people running in the manner that God designed them for. For that reason, our approach to leading has changed from trying to squeeze everyone into our box (which Steve and I are happy to live in) to allowing them to run within the lines God has drawn for them personally. Our goals are to help others discover their type and bent and do what we can to help them fulfill the things that God has created and redeemed them for.

Sometimes as leaders, we see God's calling on someone's life before they do. It's vitally important that we don't try to bypass His process of development and preparation. If we push them into being something or doing something before God's timing, it can turn serving the Lord into drudgery rather than pleasure.

The Bible declares, "We are His workmanship, created in Christ Jesus for good works, which God prepared beforehand that we should walk in them" (Ephesians 2:10). The word workmanship is the Greek word *poiéma*, from which we get our English word poem. In the first century, the meaning of the word poiéma was much broader. It referred to any type of work of art, such as a painting, a music piece, a sculpture, or even architecture. The term *workmanship* became synonymous with the term *masterpiece*. So in essence, Paul is saying that we are God's masterpiece in the making. What makes us God's masterpiece is *not* the fact that God created us, although the Bible says that we are fearfully and wonderfully made. We are God's masterpiece because He has redeemed us. The phrase "created in Christ" is the key. When we give our hearts to Jesus, we become His masterpiece in the making.

Art is the expression of the artist. Most often it reveals the artist's heart, mood, mindset, and style. The apostle Paul is telling us that God is an artist and that you and I get to be an expression of Him to the world. That is why the body of Christ is unique. It's made up of different people with different personalities and mindsets, as well as different ways of doing things. God expresses Himself in the good works that He calls us to do, which Paul declares God prepared beforehand that we should walk in them. Pastor Ray Stedman, in his commentary on the book of Ephesians, described the walk as "day by day stepping into what God has pre-ordained for our lives."[12] When I think of it that way, life gets exciting!

It also reminds me of Jesus' invitation, "Come to Me, all you who labor and are heavy laden, and I will give you rest. Take My yoke upon you and learn from Me, for I am gentle and lowly in heart, and you will find rest for your souls. For My yoke is easy and My burden is light" (Matthew 11:28–30). Many of us know how easy it is to become burdened and heavy laden in doing something that we were not created to be doing. Not only is it frustrating, it is exhausting. When Jesus says that His yoke is easy, the literal translation is that it is "well fitting." Like a pair of tailored pants, it fits perfectly when you step into it.

One of my greatest joys as a leader is to help others discover the areas where God has gifted them and where they fit perfectly. It is equally a joy and responsibility to help others discover the areas where they are weak and in need of growth or help. There is nothing better than seeing people experience God's pleasure when they run, fulfilling the things He has called them to do in that particular season.

Calvary Vista has been blessed to see some young guys mature into great pastors, Bible teachers, and worship leaders. Our hearts are full of gratitude, knowing that we were called to play a small role in their development before the Lord moved them on to impact many more lives for His kingdom.

chapter 8

Boys, Bros, & Brides

There are three constants in life ...
change, choice and principles.

Stephen Covey[13]

Stephen Covey, author of the book *The 7 Habits of Highly Effective People*, writes, "While we are free to choose our actions, we are not free to choose the consequences of our actions."[14] One area in church life where choices have long-lasting affects and consequences is in who we hire to be a part of our team. In this chapter, I want to share some of the things I have learned over the years, mistakes included, in hiring staff. I am dividing this chapter into three sections: Boys: What place in leadership should be given to young guys? Bros: Is it wise to hire men who were former senior pastors? Brides: What consideration should be given in regard to the wife of a prospective team member?

Boys

As I mentioned in the previous chapter, I have seen the Lord take some young, unproven men and grow them into great leaders and pastors. It has been a joy to watch and a privilege to be used by the Lord throughout the process. Unfortunately, though, a mistake I made more than once was not valuing their opinion or input as much as I should have. My mindset was that they were there to do a job and to be trained by our pastoral staff in preparation for the Lord to send them out. I gave young men freedom to do whatever they wanted in their own ministries, as long as it was in line with our vision to make disciples.

If they wanted to do things differently, they were welcome to ... when they started their own church. I didn't consider that they had much to offer when it came to the day-to-day functioning of the church and how we did ministry. I was the one with all the years of experience, right? Seven as a youth pastor, four as a church planter, and now leading a fairly large congregation that was making an impact in our community as well as around the world. In my mind, young guys had a lot to learn and not a lot to offer. Boy, was I wrong!

Larry Osborne, senior pastor of a megachurch in my current city of Vista, makes this observation in his book, *Sticky Teams*:

> Ironically, most churches are started by young eagles. But soon after getting their nest built, nicely appointed, and fully furnished, they start to marginalize the next batch of young eagles, asking them to sit at the kid's table and wait for their turn at middle-aged leadership. To counteract that natural tendency, I've made it a personal priority to make sure that our young eagles have a place at our leadership table. I see it as my role to enhance their influence within our church, making sure that they are supported, protected, and listened to. But I have to admit, it's not always appreciated, especially by middle-aged eagles who think that tenure should be the

primary determiner of influence. I understand their reluctance. Young eagles can make a mess in the cage. They're impatient. They lack the wisdom that comes with experience. In short, they make the same dumb mistakes that the old eagles made when they first started out.[15]

I too have learned the hard way that I need to give young eaglets a place at the table. I now have a good mixture of young men and older men on our staff and in our leadership. I love what our young guys offer and how they confront us to think in ways that we never thought before. My biggest regret is that I didn't start listening to younger men sooner. I can only imagine the difference it would have made in our church if I would have adopted this mentality several years earlier.

I would challenge any pastor who is over forty to seriously consider the generation coming up behind us. Their hearts are zealous for the Lord, with a passion for Jesus that is contagious! They are innovative and creative. They view the world through a different set of eyes and can be extremely beneficial to our churches, and us, if we are willing to listen to them. Yes, they might question the system and ask why things are being done the way they are, but that is okay, especially when they want to understand the reason why. The younger generation has a tendency to think outside the box, which is good! In the Bible, we see God often working outside the box. If, perhaps, they challenge us to break out of our comfort zone, is that really a bad thing? I, for one, am willing to welcome the challenge.

Bros

Approximately two years after I had become the pastor of Calvary Vista, I received a phone call from a friend of mine who was a pastor of a church in another state. He had been used by God to build a strong, sizable church in his particular area, but he wanted to head back to California. We talked for a while and I prayed that the Lord would give him direction. I hung up the phone and didn't think much about our call for several days. But then the thought crossed my mind that perhaps this guy, who had been a good friend and peer, would be a great addition to our team.

I thought about a role he could fill that would probably keep him busier than he was at his current church. I envisioned him overseeing our youth ministry department, our interns, and leading and teaching in our School of Discipleship and Ministry. I could also give him the opportunity to fill the pulpit for me when I was away on vacations, missions' trips, or speaking at conferences, all of which took me out of the pulpit four to six times per year. I believed there was potential for him to eventually move into the role of being my #2 pastor because, at that time, a group of guys all shared various aspects of that responsibility.

I took a couple of days to pray and felt a peace about at least exploring the possibility with him, so I decided to give him a call. I asked him if he could ever see himself going back into a staff role at another church, or if he felt he was only called to be a senior pastor. I knew guys who recognized that they could never go back to being an assistant pastor once they had tasted the freedom and responsibility of being the lead guy in their own church. He replied that in the right situation and in a bigger church, he would have no problem being in an assistant role again. So I told him what I was thinking and asked him to take a few days to pray and talk to his wife. If they were interested, they could come for a visit, and we could talk face to face about the possibility.

He and his wife were very interested in making the move to Vista, so we scheduled a trip for him to come down. He sat in a few services and staff meetings and got a taste of what the Lord was doing at the time. He was extremely excited about what he saw. I invited him over to the house to have dinner and to give my wife a chance to meet him because she has always had great discernment about things and people. After he left that evening, my wife said to me, "I don't have a peace about this; something doesn't seem right." The mistake I made was ignoring her concern. I told her she would see that he was a great guy who would be a real asset to our church.

The next day I made him a formal offer to come down and join our team. He accepted and went back home to set in motion his move to Vista. Approximately two months later, he was at the church and had started to assume his responsibilities. What happened next absolutely caught me off guard. One day, after only being with us for a couple of months, he pulled me aside and told me that he had made a wrong decision and that he needed to be a senior pastor. Here we had opened up our doors, created ministry opportunities for him, and helped pay to move his family to California to become a part of our team. Now, only eight weeks at the job, he informed me that he was going to look for a place to plant a church or find a church that needed a senior pastor.

Hindsight is always 20/20. If I had it to do all over again, I would have cut my losses, given him a small severance out of grace, and sent him on his way. Instead, I allowed him to stay on staff until he figured out what he was going to do next. That ended up taking nearly a year, creating church strife and personal stress on me.

So this brings me back to my question: Should you ever hire a former senior pastor to join your staff? Well, it took me thirteen years to even consider doing that again. But eventually, I invited a former staff member, Jason Duff, back to Calvary Vista. This is a man who is fifteen years younger than I am and had previously served on my staff for seven years as the high school youth pastor. During that time he did an excellent job leading our high school ministry, and through his leadership, it grew to the largest it had been in years. He then moved to Texas to take over a church there and pastored that growing fellowship for about six years. During the time that Jason had been away, we stayed in touch, roomed together at the annual Senior Pastors Conference, and when he was in town, I usually gave him an opportunity to teach at our church, where he was always warmly received. When I invited him to pray about coming back as a teaching pastor, he shared with me that when he had left Vista, the Lord had spoke to him that one day he was going to return, and he and I were going to minister together again.

I invited Jason back for a specific purpose. In the thirty years that Calvary Vista had been in existence, there were only two primary voices from the pulpit—Pastor Brian Brodersen and myself. Sure, there were guest speakers who would come and share, but I felt it was time for another voice. I had noticed several other ministries over the years that had gone to a team-teaching format, including Larry Osborne and Chris Brown, who were setting an awesome example of this in my own town. I saw the benefit of what a young, teaching pastor could bring to our church at its stage in history.

The difference in this scenario from the previous one is that Jason has always seen me as his pastor and has had a great love and respect for my family and me. Jason is also aware of the areas where I am strong, and he has sought to merely compliment me in the areas where I am weak rather than exploit my weaknesses. I think the fact that I have given Jason a lot of freedom in his schedule and the opportunity to do what he loves to do, which is teach the Bible, has brought forth fruit. Weekly communication and prayer has also been a key factor in making this scenario work. I feel that both of us are ministering in an area where we are in our "wheel house," so to speak. The church body has been blessed by hearing from both of us, and we have seen the church grow as a result of this new direction. The extra freedom in my schedule has allowed me to strengthen some areas of our ministry that previously had been neglected and spend quality time with my staff.

To sum up this section on whether or not it is a good idea to hire a former senior pastor, I would say that I think it can work, but proceed with caution. And when your wife says she doesn't have a good feeling about it, by all means, listen to her!

Brides

When it comes to the subject of hiring a guy to fill the role of an assistant pastor, should you take into consideration the character and spiritual maturity of his wife? Absolutely! Isn't it good enough that she loves the Lord and is a Christian? No. Paul the apostle, when speaking about the wife of a deacon, says in 1 Timothy 3:11, "Likewise, their wives must be reverent, not slanderers, temperate, faithful in all things." What Paul says about the wife of a deacon is equally as important concerning the wife of an assistant pastor. She must be a woman of good character who is spiritually mature, able to control her tongue, and a faithful wife, mother, and church member.

When looking at men who I thought had the potential to join our staff or our leadership team, I wrongly assumed that if the guy was godly and mature, his wife was too. If he was passionate about ministry, she would be also. This false assumption led to a few difficult situations where I eventually discovered the wife was not supportive of her husband's calling or she was not spiritually mature or prepared to be a pastor's wife. Discontentment over the sacrifice, the pay, the hours, the commitment, and the expectations created conflict and challenges.

Being a pastor's wife is an unusual calling:

• The wife of a pastor has to share her husband with a lot of other people; therefore, she needs to know that God has called her. Her husband needs to be confident that she is ready for that level of commitment and sacrifice.

• The wife of a pastor often functions like a single mother in regard to attending church services, especially where there are multiple services. Chances are, her husband will be required to be at the church long before the services start. On most Sundays, she will get the kids ready for church on her own, drive to and from church by herself, and depending on what her husband's responsibilities are, she might be sitting in the service alone. If there is an evening service, she most likely will return home to an empty house and put the kids to bed by herself.

• There are also the unfair expectations that people put on pastor's wives. It is assumed that she will be available, have all the answers, is able to counsel, attends all the functions, and has well behaved, "perfect" children, just to mention a few.

An Assistant Pastor's Wife Is a Part of the Team

I really didn't contemplate early on in ministry that when a man joined our team, that his wife would have influence. For that reason alone, it is extremely important that she is on board with the vision and leadership of the church and has a respect for you as the pastor and for your wife as your partner in ministry. Now, that doesn't mean that you and your wife need to be best friends with the couples on your ministry team or spend countless hours hanging out together, but there needs to be a respect and realization that they are called to serve Jesus alongside you and your bride.

The reality is, sheep follow their leaders, and if an assistant pastor's wife shows signs of being disgruntled, other disgruntled people will gravitate to her. She has to be spiritually mature and submitted to her husband, the Lord, and the church to graciously handle the role she has and all of the emotions and situations that go along with it.

So How Do You Determine if She is Ready?

There is no foolproof way to tell if a wife is ready for the calling of a pastor's wife. But here are some suggestions and a few things I have implemented that have helped us when considering hiring a man for a position.

- If the wife has served in any ministry capacity in the church, talk to the leaders that she has served with. What is her reputation? Is she humble? Is she respected? Does she slander others? Does she exercise self-control with her tongue? Is she faithful in the area of ministry she serves in (1 Timothy 3:11)? Is she a team player? Does she exhibit a servant's heart and a heart for people?

- Don't just interview the husband, but plan a session where you bring them in together or take them to lunch. Every pastor knows the ministry culture of his church, and it is important to determine if someone will be a good fit for that culture.

For instance, at Calvary Vista, almost everyone on staff has more than one major responsibility, and some have as many as three. Therefore, I have learned the importance of painting a realistic view of ministry culture and expectations that will be upon the man who is being considered for an assistant pastor position. I have learned to pay attention to body language and the tone in someone's voice when they respond. I look for negative reactions and push backs, especially from the wife, when discussing these aspects of our ministry. If I pick up on these, it will raise an immediate red flag in my heart. I think it is crucial for the wife, as well as the husband, to clearly understand what full-time ministry at Calvary Vista requires and be on board, with God's grace, to fulfill that calling.

• If the wife is not ready to step into this role, it doesn't mean that you might not ever hire her husband, or that her husband is not called to full-time ministry, but it might not be the right time or the right place. They might be a perfect fit in another ministry culture.

Successful ministry happens when you have the right people at the right place at the right time. I have found that when all three are lined up, things work a lot better. I admit this is a hard thing to do, especially when you have a spot to fill and you see a guy who would be an awesome fit. But it's worth the wait; trust God to provide in His perfect time and will.

I have a dear friend who I believe would make a great pastor at any level. He is wise, a gifted teacher, godly, and an amazing man of integrity and wisdom. But he told me years ago that he wasn't sure his wife was ready or called to that lifestyle, so he was going to look for ways to use his gifts in the body of Christ a different way. He has done that and God has used him in incredible ways over the years in his church, all the while working in secular environments. He is a wise man, as is any man who has his identity in Christ and not in a position in the church.

So when it comes to boys, give them a voice! When it comes to bros, pray really hard in considering if someone is ready to step into that type of role. When it comes to brides, paint a clear picture and do your homework, and remember that timing is everything!

chapter 9

Less Is More

Someday you will be old enough to start reading fairy tales again.

C. S. LEWIS[16]

As a young boy, I found it fascinating to watch my dad shave his face. He would lather up with that old school Barbasol shaving cream, and then, with careful strokes of his metal shaver, his whiskers would vanish away. I would stare at him, fascinated by how cool I thought that was. One day, when I was about six years old, I climbed onto the bathroom counter, reached into the cabinet, and took out my dad's shaving cream and razor. I pressed the button on the can and out squirted the cream—all over my hands. I smeared it on my face, grabbed the razor, and started to swipe. OUCH! Suddenly, there was blood flowing down my cheeks and onto the bathroom floor. I grabbed a towel and ran out of the bathroom, crying for my mom. When she asked me what had happened, I answered with extreme pain in my voice, "I cut myself shaving!"

I am sure that many men have a similar story from when they were children. Why do little boys want so badly to shave? Because in the heart of every little guy, there is a longing to be grown up!

A Longing to be "Legit"

I believe every church planter has a similar aspiration. We didn't come to play church. We set out to have a bona fide, "legit" ministry as soon as possible. At one time in the movement that I am a part of, in order to be considered a church, you needed to meet in a location other than a home, or else you were acknowledged as a "home fellowship" on the affiliation list and not a church. No one wanted to stay on that list very long.

Nowadays, because of our media-driven culture and the advancement of technology, there is added pressure to appear more together than you really are. I have heard it said at conferences and stated in articles that if people don't like your website, they will not visit your church! I have seen some church planters venture out with cool business cards and an impressive website before they have even launched their first service. The church website lists staff members, Bible studies, blogs, and more, giving the illusion of an established church. But when people show up, they discover that the reality is not what was presented on the website. That can be counterproductive, especially if it is interpreted as being disingenuous.

I believe a new church plant should seek to have a clean and attractive website, but it needs to be honest. Don't be afraid to let people know who and what you are in a simple and forthright manner. Beware of trying to grow up too fast. People are looking for churches that are authentic.

A Full Schedule

In our church plant, my longing to be legit affected my approach—we needed to have a full schedule as quickly as possible. In my mind, a "real church" had a lot of things going on; and if I was going to print a church bulletin, then I needed to have things to put in it. So in addition to Sunday morning services, we had a Wednesday night Bible study (never mind that there were only three people present, and two of them were in my own family!). We had a weekly women's prayer meeting and a Saturday morning men's study. (In actuality, that Saturday morning men's study was the best thing that I ever did, and I will explain why at the end of the chapter.) The point I am trying to make is that I subconsciously thought that the more we did, the more legit we were as a church and the more opportunity we had to grow.

Sharpshooters Versus a Shotgun Blast

My way of thinking changed abruptly after Jon Courson shared his convictions with me on this matter. He explained that many Christians and churches approach ministry like a shotgun blast. They are doing so many things and making little tiny dents in a whole bunch of areas. But Jon believes that in these last days, God is looking for Christians and churches to be more like sharpshooters, making a big dent in one or two areas.

In other words, less is sometimes more. For that reason, I now encourage guys, when they are starting out as a new church plant, to focus on doing one thing really well. If I had it to do all over again, I would have concentrated on the Sunday morning service and would not have implemented a midweek study until there was a need for it. Be a sharpshooter and have as big of an impact as you possibly can for the kingdom.

Calvary Chapel Corvallis

A church that has set a great example of this "less is more" concept is Calvary Chapel Corvallis in Corvallis, Oregon. During my last year in Oregon, there was a group of people driving an hour to our church from the college town of Corvallis. Ironically, this was the area I had originally wanted to plant our church in but discovered Calvary Chapel was already starting there, and I was encouraged to go elsewhere. Unfortunately, the church in Corvallis ended up having two pastors in a three-year period, and the current pastor was struggling with his doctrine and calling. So five or six families began driving to our church on Sunday mornings and sometimes on Wednesday nights.

Eventually, the pastor called to tell me that he was moving on and asked if I would help him find a new pastor for the church. After I hung up the phone, I immediately thought of my friend Rob Verdeyen—a great Bible teacher and strong leader who was the current high school pastor at Calvary Chapel Costa Mesa. I called Rob and told him Corvallis was ripe for God to do something amazing. My wife and I love Rob and his wife, Susie, and envisioned ministering an hour away from each other. We could do men's and women's retreats, family camps, and youth conferences for years to come. Rob and Susie prayed and then traveled to Corvallis to meet with the small group of about twenty-five people, which included some of the families from our church. The Verdeyens made the decision to take a huge step of faith, leaving sunny California to come to Oregon and shepherd the church.

Although Rob came from a large, active church that had several things happening every night of the week, he seemed to instinctively understand that less is more. Rob started with two things—a Saturday night prayer meeting for anyone who wanted to come and a Sunday morning service. Today, Calvary Corvallis is a church of approximately two thousand people, with an over 56-acre campus that God provided. Although they eventually added other ministries and activities, the Saturday night prayer meeting and the Sunday service are still, to this day, the backbone of the church.

If I were starting over again, I would do exactly what Rob Verdeyen did. Establishing the church with a weekly prayer meeting is one of the smartest choices, I personally believe, that you can make. Less is more is a powerful concept that allows you to focus on the things that are the most important and to do those things well.

Less Is More Applies to Teaching

I have to admit that after spending close to ten years teaching youth, including my volunteer time at Calvary Chapel Costa Mesa, I was eager to have the opportunity to teach adults. I was so eager that I tried to feed them a full course meal at every sitting. My studies were long and packed with enough information for two or three studies. I wanted to share everything that I had read or heard or felt like the Lord had showed me.

Recently, I pulled out some hard copies of my early teachings, and to be honest, I can't believe people sat through those sermons. They weren't bad, just excessive.

It doesn't matter how good the turkey, stuffing, mashed potatoes, and desserts are at a Thanksgiving meal; too much of a good thing can turn into a bad thing.

I have learned over the years of teaching weekly Bible studies that there is wisdom in saying less and repeating more, because people forget. The apostle Peter put it this way, "I think it is right, as long as I am in this body, to stir you up by way of reminder" (2 Peter 1:13, ESV).

A Growing Attention Span

Now, I am not one who believes people have small attention spans or that a congregation can only handle fifteen- to twenty-minute sermons. It has been my experience that a person's attention span can grow over time, if approached the right way. A pastor who forms well thought-out outlines, accompanied with illustrations that bring clarity to the point, will find this to be true. I love it when someone comes up after a forty-five- to fifty-minute message and says that the time just flew by or that they wanted to hear more.

When I prepare a sermon, I want to address three things within the covered text. First, I look for what I like to call the MILK—the point in the text that shares the gospel or gives me a launching pad from which to share it. The place it is shared in the message may vary. It might be in the beginning, middle, or end. But wherever its located, ninety percent of the time I will refer back to the milk at the end of the study, giving people the opportunity to respond to the gospel.

The second aspect I look for is the MEAT—the "who, what, and when" of the text. The meat represents the context and the doctrine presented in the passage—how it connects to the rest of the book and the message of the Bible as a whole. I spend a good portion of the sermon on the meat of the text for the body.

After I have accurately dissected the passage, I am ready to share the third element, which I call the MANNA. The manna is a specific word from the Lord for the church on that day. It is often the point of application for us to pray in and think through. This, to me, is the most important part of teaching and is frequently the last thing impressed upon my heart in the preparation process. However, there are occasions when the Lord gives me this first. But everything in the message is building toward the delivery of that "word from the Lord" for that particular day or season in the life of the church. Ninety percent of the time, we teach expositionally at our church. I have found that as we go through an entire book of the Bible, there will be five to ten specific exhortations or truths as manna from the Lord.

Having a concrete method of study has really helped me, as a teacher, to concentrate and communicate what I need to say as clearly as possible. It has also kept me from repeating myself, using the same four or five different stories or analogies over and over again. Preachers are notorious for this. We call it being verbose, but verbose can often be boring and leave people feeling as if they have been force-fed. I think we have all heard a sermon or read a book where we find ourselves saying, "Okay, I get the point! You can move on now." And lest I start heading down that road, I am going to wrap up this chapter by sharing the reason why having a Saturday morning men's group was such a great thing for me as a leader and for our church as a whole.

Discovering the Spiritual Makeup of the Men in Your Church

When I began the men's group, I rarely taught because I didn't have time to prepare another Bible study. This gave me an opportunity to use books as a tool to effectively communicate subject matters that were on my heart for our church. For instance, when I wanted to convey the subject of servant leadership, I asked the men to read Gayle Erwin's *The Jesus Style*. It is by far the best book I have ever read on that subject. If I wanted the guys to learn about prayer, we would read a book by Andrew Murray. I would have the men read a chapter or two during the week and come prepared on Saturdays to share what God had spoken to them or put upon their hearts.

Here is why I think this was brilliant, if I do say so myself! (I know this book is about mistakes I have made in ministry, but after nine chapters of laying out all the things I have done wrong, indulge me on this one.) By having the men participate in this format, I learned which guys were spiritually disciplined. They were the guys who read the chapters and came ready to share. I also discovered which guys potentially had the gift of teaching. They were the ones who could articulate their thoughts in a way that made sense and was impactful. Some of them had good, scriptural insight and were able to build upon what the author had said by linking it to some other portion of Scripture. But I was also able to perceive which guys were lazy, or at least lacked spiritual discipline in their lives. They perpetually had excuses for not reading the material but enjoyed coming to be with the guys. There were also a few pretenders who obviously had not done the homework, but they wanted us to think they had by sharing something that they thought would be related to the chapter.

My point is this: our particular study format became an excellent way to find out the spiritual makeup of the men in our church; and it gave us insight and discernment in assigning leadership roles and responsibilities. I have continued over the years to use this method of training with men's groups, our staff and leadership, and with select groups of men in our church in whom I see a potential for future leadership or service. Reading a book together and talking about it each week has helped our staff stay on the same page as it relates to our vision. It has also been beneficial for my leadership team to better capture the things that God has placed on my heart.

Throughout the years of ministry, I have persisted in looking for more effective ways to communicate, especially in small group settings. My desire is to help keep our church fixed on being sharpshooters, unified in our passion to reach people with the gospel, and to see people grow in the grace and knowledge of our Lord Jesus Christ. We are continuing to discover that sometimes less is definitely more, and deep is better than wide.

CONCLUSION

I believe the single greatest way to reach a community is to plant a church. The gospel is the power of God unto salvation to whoever believes, so it needs to be preached! Isn't it amazing that our God, who spoke the universe into existence and sent His beloved Son to earth to pay a ransom for many, has chosen people to partner with Him in His redemptive plan to reach a lost and dying world? He has done the work, and He has commissioned us to share the message.

One of the great passions of my life is to sit down with young men who desire to go out and plant churches because I love God's people and I love the lost! My heart is to see men minister as effectively as they possibly can without being sidetracked. I pray that this book has been helpful—that you have been reassured of your calling and encouraged to keep going. Never grow weary in well doing, because in due season, you will reap if you do not lose heart (Galatians 6:9)! God loves you so much, and He is with you and for you. Learn to live life fully dependent upon the empowering and leading of His Holy Spirit—He *will* enable you to do exactly what He has called you to do for His glory! I leave you with this thought from 1 Corinthians 15:58 (ESV):

> Therefore, my beloved brothers, be steadfast, immovable, always abounding in the work of the Lord, knowing that in the Lord your labor is not in vain.

ABOUT THE AUTHOR

Rob Salvato is the lead pastor at Calvary Vista in Southern California.

He has served in this position since 1996. Prior to that, Rob planted a church in northern Oregon called Calvary Chapel Christian Fellowship, which he was the pastor of for five years. Before church planting, Rob served for seven years in various positions of youth ministry at Calvary Vista.

He is happily married to his best friend, Denise, and they have three adult children. Pastor Rob has a passion for God's Word and for men called into full-time ministry. He regularly speaks at churches and conferences around the world. His radio program, "The Basics of Life," can be heard on radio stations around the United States and in New Zealand.

NOTES

[1] Donald Grey Barnhouse, *Romans: 2 Volumes* (Grand Rapids, MI: Eerdmans Publishing, 1982).

[2] Ibid.

[3] Ibid.

[4] John Donne, *The Works of John Donne. vol III.* Henry Alford, ed. (London: John W. Parker, 1839).

[5] Warren W. Wiersbe, *The Bumps Are What You Climb On* (Michigan: Baker, 2006).

[6] http://www.brainyquote.com/quotes/authors/r/ron_jaworski.html.

[7] http://m.ccel.org/ccel/spurgeon/sermons37.xxxv.html.

[8] Søren Kierkegaard, *Journalen* JJ:167 (1843), Søren Kierkegaard Research Center, Copenhagen, 1997--, volume 18, page 306.

[9] Paul David Tripp, *A Quest for More: Living for Something Bigger Than You* (North Carolina: New Growth Press, 2007).

[10] Charles R. Swindoll, *Jesus: The Greatest Life of All* (Great Life Series) (Nashville, TN: Thomas Nelson, 2008).

[11] Crawford Loritts, *Leadership as an Identity: The Four Traits of Those Who Wield Lasting Influence* (Chicago, IL: Moody, 2009).

[12] Ray C. Stedman, *Our Riches in Christ: Discovering the Believer's Inheritance in Ephesians* (Ontario: Discovery House Publishers, 1998).

[13] Stephen R. Covey, *The 7 Habits of Highly Effective People* (New York, NY: Free Press, 1987).

[14] Ibid.

[15] Larry Osborne, *Sticky Teams: Keeping Your Leadership Team and Staff on the Same Page* (Nashville, TN: Zondervan, 2010).

[16] C. S. Lewis, *The Lion, The Witch, and the Wardrobe* (London: Geoffrey Bles, 1950).

Made in the USA
Charleston, SC
20 September 2014